Lizard Lumps, Burps, and Bumps?

Fascinating Lizard Facts

Photos by Bob Ferguson II

Written by Jessica Lee Anderson

Paperback ISBN: 978-1-964078-58-8

To my nephew, Zachary, and my niece, Jill, I've always loved finding lizards with you, and I'm so grateful for you both along with your families! - JLA

To my stepson, Zach - Since our first trip to the Pine Barrens in 2008 to our recent trip in Thailand, you have proven over and over again, nobody can catch lizards like you! - BF

All photos taken by Bob Ferguson II apart from P. 4: Beautifulblossom (Tuatara); P.6: JNemchinova (Lizard fossil); P. 8: emer1940 (Slow Worm); P. 9: Billion Photos (Bearded Dragon), seb868 (Chinese Water Dragon); P. 14: John Carnemolla (Yellow-spotted Monitor); P. 17: WagnerJames (Blue-Tongued Skink); P. 19: tane-mahuta (Gold Tegu) P. 20: rick734's Images (Coast Horned Lizard); P. 21: NNehring (San Esteban Chuckwalla); P. 24: Tourism Australia (Frilled-Neck Lizard); P. 28: Kaan Sezer (African Fat-tailed Gecko); P. 30: Andrey Gudkov (Komodo Dragon); P. 31: Miropa (Thorny Devil)

Names of species (current iNaturalist common names) clockwise from top left, unless otherwise noted: Front cover: Eastern Collared Lizard; Title Page: Argentine Black and White Tegu; Copyright Page: Tokay Gecko; Dedication: Casque-headed Iguana; P. 4: American Alligator, Tuatara, Southern Alligator Lizard; P. 5: Northern Curly-Tailed Lizard, Tree Runner, Yellow-headed Gecko; P. 6: Helmeted Iguana, Five-lined Skink, Lizard Fossil; P. 7: Amazon Forest Dragon, Desert Spiny Lizard, Gila Monster; P. 8: Slender Glass Lizard Island Glass Lizard, Slow Worm; P. 9: Amazon Forest Dragon, Bearded Dragon, Chinese Water Dragon; P. 10: Gliding Gecko foot close-up, Tokay Gecko foot close-up, Yucatan Banded Gecko, Madagascar Giant Day Gecko, Western Banded Gecko; P. 11: Setaro Dwarf Chameleon, Montane Side-striped Chameleons, Veiled Chameleon; P. 12: Black Spiny Tailed Lizard, Broad-headed Wood Lizard, Green Iguana; P. 13: Green Anole, Banded Tree Anole, Inhering's Fathead Anole; P. 14: Yellow-spotted monitor, Clouded Monitor, Nile Monitor; P. 15: Eastern Fence Lizard, Granite Spiny Lizard, Slevin's Bunchgrass Lizard; P. 16: Western Basilisk, Emerald Basilisk, Brown Basilisk; P. 17: Striped Litter Skink, Five-lined Skink with eggs, Blue-tongued Skink; P. 18: Forest Whiptail, Amazon Whiptail, Rainbow Whiptail; P. 19: Gold Tegu, Argentine Black and White Tegu (adult and baby); P. 20: Texas Horned Lizard, Coast Horned Lizard, Regal Horned Lizard; P: 21: Chuckwalla, San Esteban Chuckwalla, Chuckwalla; P. 22: Red-eyed Wood Lizard, Eastern Collared Lizard, Montane Side-striped Chameleon; P. 23: Yellow-spotted spiny lizard, Striped Skink, Black Spiny-tailed Iguana; P. 24: Green Iguana, Frilled-Neck Lizard, Southern Turnip-tail Gecko; P. 25: Collared Lizard, Gila Monster, Spinytail Iguana; P. 26: Desert Banded Gecko, American Crow eating Island Glass Lizard, Northern Scarletsnake and Five-lined Skink; P. 27: Hippie Anole, Spinytail Iguna, Common Monkey Lizard; P. 28: Brown Basilisk, Granite Night Lizard; P. 29: Yucatan Spiny-tailed Iguana, Lichen Anole; Ameiva; P. 30: Komodo Dragon, Surpise Anole, Green Iguna,; P. 31: Thorny Devil, Red-headed Agama, Surprise Anole, P. 32: Veiled Chameleons; Back cover: Veiled Chameleoen

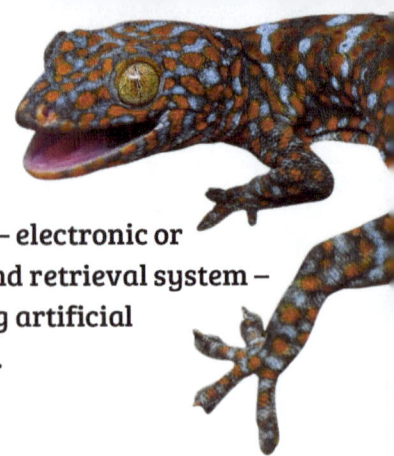

This Book Belongs to:

_____

Differences Between Lizards and Alligators

American alligator

A tuatara may look like a lizard, though it is a very unique reptile in an order on its own!

Lizards are reptiles with scales and tails (though some species can drop them), and they usually have four limbs. While alligators and crocodiles are reptiles that look similar to lizards, they have different features and ancestors. They belong to separate taxonomy groups called orders. Lizards (and snakes too) belong to the order Squamata while alligators belong to the order Crocodilia.

Alligator lizard

"Cold-Blooded"

Lizard species are diverse and can be found in a variety of environments. Like all reptiles, lizards are "cold-blooded" (though biologists use terms like ectothermic or poikilothermic). Lizards rely on the environment to stay the right temperature, which is why they often bask in sunny spots on rocks or on branches.

The body temperature of a lizard changes—it does not mean that their blood is cold to the touch.

Bones and Fossils

Reptiles like lizards breathe air and have scales instead of fur or feathers. They are known as vertebrates because they have backbones.

Lizards have existed since ancient times! Researchers have discovered different kinds of lizard fossils from the past. Lizards lived during the time of dinosaurs, but they are not closely related together.

Scales, Lumps, and Bumps

Lizards can have different types and sizes of scales that vary by species. Scales provide protection from predators and from the sun. They are made from keratin, the same protein that forms your skin and hair. Scales can vary in texture from smooth to bumpy (granular). Some scales are keeled, meaning a ridge runs down the center of them, giving the lizard a dry, rough look. Certain lizard species have lumpy looking bony plates called osteoderms for protection.

The scales on a lizard are not all identical—they can vary in size and shape on different parts of the body.

Legless Lizards?

There are groups of lizards that resemble snakes because they don't have any limbs (or if they do, they're tiny and don't function like legs). Unlike snakes, legless lizards and slow worms have eyelids that move and visible ear holes. They also have differences in their skull structure and tongues, plus they can't open their jaws as wide as snakes do when they eat.

Legless lizards move side-to-side and don't move in a fluid, smooth motion like snakes as they lack the same kind of belly scales.

Dragons

Many lizard species are called dragons such Amazon forest dragons, bearded dragons, Chinese water dragons, and more. These real-life reptiles resemble mythical dragons. Several of the dragon lizards are in the Agamidae family. Agamids have unique teeth on the edge of their jaw, and they generally don't drop their tails if they sense a threat.

Bearded dragons have spiky beards that can puff up and turn black if they become stressed.

Geckos

Unlike other lizard species, geckos can make sounds like barks, chirps, clicks, squeals, and squeaks. Many geckos have special toe pads that help them to cling to a variety of surfaces. While most geckos are nocturnal (active at night), species like day geckos are diurnal (active during the day).

Many species of geckos and other lizards can drop their tails (autotomy) as a way to escape predators.

Chameleons

Chameleons are different than other lizards because of the shape of their feet and body, the way their eyes move, and their long, sticky tongues. Chameleons commonly dwell in trees (arboreal), and many species have prehensile tails that they use to grasp branches as they climb.

Iguanas

Iguanas and dwarf iguana species have small "spikes" (called dorsal spines) along their bodies as well as a flap under their neck called a dewlap. Dorsal spines and dewlaps can be used to display aggression or dominance.

Anoles

Anoles are closely related to iguanas, and many species have "sticky" toe pads like geckos. Unlike geckos, all species of anoles have moveable eyelids, plus they are primarily diurnal. Several species of anoles have adapted to living in urban areas.

Monitors

Monitors are a type of lizard with a thick body, powerful legs, and a long neck and tail. They can stand on their hind legs to look around, "monitoring" the surroundings around them.

Spiny Lizards

Spiny lizards have a spiny appearance because of sharp-pointed, keeled scales. They're commonly seen in the United States. Their toes and claws help them climb rocky habitats.

Basilisks

Basilisks are semi-aquatic, meaning they live on land and in the water. They have interesting feet and long toes that allow them to run on water!

Skinks

In general, skinks have thicker necks, shorter legs, and longer bodies compared to other types of lizards. Several lizard species like blue-tongued skinks give birth to live young (viviparous), though the vast majority of lizards lay eggs (oviparous). Depending on the species and the temperature, eggs typically take about one to four months to hatch.

Whiptails

As you might guess from the name, whiptail lizards have long whip-like tails. They have slender bodies with pointed heads. Whiptails are mostly terrestrial (ground dwelling), like the vast majority of lizard species.

Tegus

Tegus are in the same family as whiptails (Teiidae). Tegus tend to be bigger and eat larger prey items like rodents. Studies have shown that tegus are intelligent!

Horned Lizards

Horned lizards have a crown of horn-like bony scales on their heads that protect them against predators. They can squirt nasty-tasting blood from their eyes to discourage predators like coyotes! Horned lizards live in prairie and desert habitats in North America.

Chuckwallas

Chuckwallas dwell in the harsh desert. They're herbivores and don't drink water often because they get what they need from the plants they eat. Chuckwallas even have a special way of storing water in their body.

Colors and Patterns

There are many other kinds of lizards! Lizards come in a wide variety of colors from brown to vibrant greens, reds, yellows, blues, and mixes of different colors. Even the eye colors of lizards can widely vary depending on the species! Some species like chameleons and anoles have the ability to change colors! Patterns can be diverse as well, such as bands, speckles, and stripes.

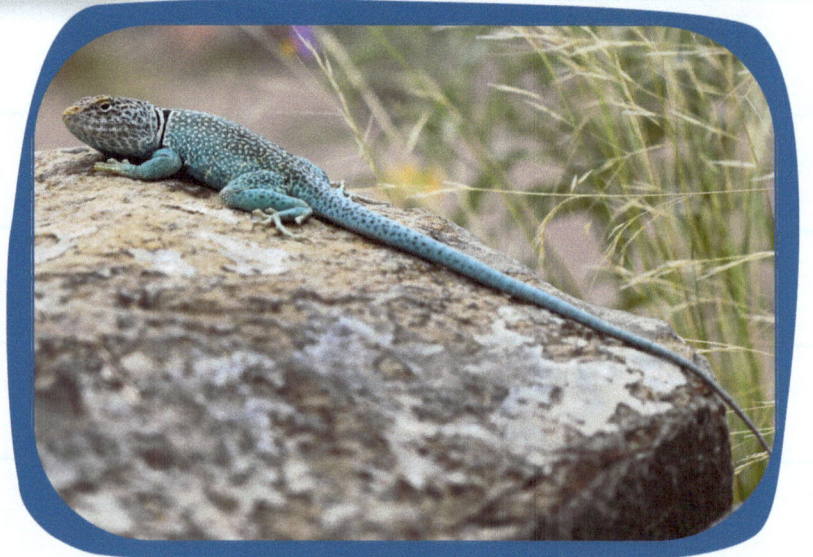

Camouflage

Camouflage adaptations like colors, patterns, and special features help lizards blend into their environment and go unnoticed by potential predators (such as birds of prey, other reptiles, and mammals). Camouflage also makes it easier for lizards to hunt.

Communication

Geckos vocalize to communicate, though other lizard species are capable of hissing, especially if they sense a threat. Lizards also communicate through body language, such as head bobs, push-ups, and extending dorsal spines, dewlaps, or frills. Lizards can secrete chemicals called pheromones from special glands to communicate as well.

Defense

In addition to camouflage, body language, and hissing, lizards have other methods of defense like mouth gaping, tail whipping, and/or striking. Venomous lizards use venom, a toxic secretion made from protein and chemicals, as a tool for hunting and defense. Researchers studied Gila monster venom to develop human medications to treat diabetes.

Predators or Prey?

Lizards are both predators and prey! Some lizards eat fruit, nectar, and plants, while others prey on insects, rodents, amphibians, and more. Lizards keep populations of pests in check. Predators like mammals, other reptiles, and birds of prey rely upon lizards for survival.

Burps?

Lizards can take up to a week to digest their food, and they can have troubles if the environment is too hot or cold. Some lizards will burp if they swallow air or if they are having digestive issues. Lizards can get respiratory infections and might make sounds similar to burping if they're ill.

Amazing Adaptations

Some geckos store fat in their tails, an adaptation that helps them survive if food becomes scarce.

Many lizards have well-developed senses that help them to find food and escape predators. Lizards generally have good hearing, especially those with external ear openings. Research has shown that some lizard species have better vision than humans and that some nocturnal species can see color vision at night!

Survival Strategies

Lizards are excellent at hiding to survive, and some will dig burrows. In cold climates, certain lizards seek shelter and slow down in a process called brumation. Brumation is similar to hibernation, though lizards still have some activity. Lizards can survive months without food!

From Mini to Massive

There are around 7,000 lizard species found all over the globe, apart from Antarctica! Lizards vary in size and weight. Some lizards are about the length of a paperclip while many other lizards are longer than an adult human's arm. The largest species, Komodo dragons, can be as long as a surfboard and can weigh more than some human adults!

Legendary Lizards

Australia has the highest number of lizard species (over 800 have been recorded)!

Scientists are continuing to learn more about lizards as well as discover new species! Lizards are an important, essential part of our world.

Jessica Lee Anderson is an award-winning author of over 100 books for young readers including the NAOMI NASH chapter book series. Jessica loves spending time in nature and exploring the outdoors with her husband, Michael, and their daughter, Ava! She also enjoys bearded dragon sitting for friends. You can learn more about Jessica by visiting www.jessicaleeanderson.com.

Bob is a naturalist with a compulsion to be outdoors. Wildlife conservation through entertainment, education, fundraising, and fieldwork is his mission and purpose in life. His organization, Fascinature, has donated six figures to saving land in the world's most biodiverse spaces. He even has a frog named after him! You can find him on Instagram @bob_ferguson_fascinature or sign up for his newsletter at fascinature.live.

Check out these other books!

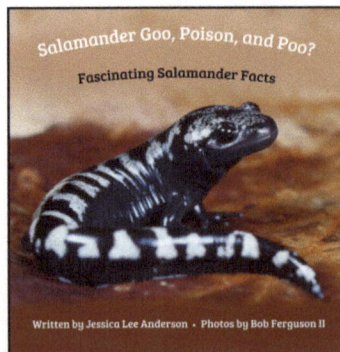

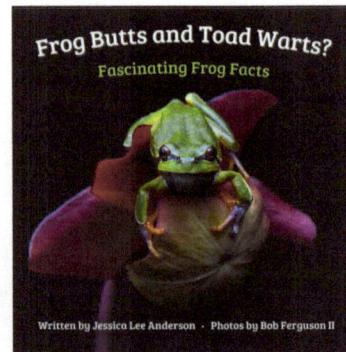

Turtle Snoots, Scutes, and Toots?
Fascinating Turtle Facts
Written by Jessica Lee Anderson · Photos by Bob Ferguson II

Salamander Goo, Poison, and Poo?
Fascinating Salamander Facts
Written by Jessica Lee Anderson · Photos by Bob Ferguson II

Frog Butts and Toad Warts?
Fascinating Frog Facts
Written by Jessica Lee Anderson · Photos by Bob Ferguson II

www.ingramcontent.com/pod-product-compliance
Lightning Source LLC
Chambersburg PA
CBHW061145030426

42335CB00002B/113